Walt Disney's
Pooh and Piglet's Book of Big and Little

GOLDEN PRESS • NEW YORK
WESTERN PUBLISHING COMPANY, INC.
RACINE, WISCONSIN

Copyright © 1979 by Walt Disney Productions. All rights reserved.
No part of this book may be reproduced or copied in any form without written permission from the copyright owner.
Printed in the U.S.A. by Western Publishing Company, Inc.
GOLDEN®, A GOLDEN BOOK®, and GOLDEN PRESS® are trademarks of Western Publishing Company, Inc.
Library of Congress Catalog Card Number: 79-63297
ISBN 0-307-12368-5

Contents

Yes and No	3
Fast and Slow	4
Full and Empty	6
Front and Back	8
Up and Down	10
Smooth and Rough	14
Top and Bottom	16
Wet and Dry	21
Hot and Cold	22
Soft and Hard	24
Sick and Well	25
In and Out	26
Over and Under	28
Big and Little	30
Old and New	34
High and Low	35
Mad and Glad	40
Happy and Sad	41
Quiet and Noisy	42
First and Last	44
Day and Night	48

Pooh's Yes and No Song

Do I love to eat
Lots of honey?
Well, just guess—
The answer is **yes**.

Do I like it when
The honey pot's empty?
Ho, ho, ho—
The answer is **no**.

Fast and Slow

The race is on—
Crawl, creep, scurry!
Here they come—
Hop, run, hurry!

The race is on—
Just look at them go!
Some, like Tigger, are **fast**
And some, like Eeyore, are **slow.**

As **fast** as Owl,
blinking his eye...

As **slow** as Eeyore,
sighing a sigh...

As **fast** as Rabbit,
winning a race...

As **slow** as Roo,
washing his face!

Full and Empty

Three **full** honey jars
Standing in a row...

Now they are **empty**—
Where did the honey go?

I know!

Is Christopher Robin's juice glass **empty** or **full**?

Is Pooh's wagon **empty** or **full**?

Is Kanga's pouch **full** or **empty**?

Is Rabbit's cupboard **full** or **empty**?

Front and Back

This is what Pooh and his friends all look like from the **front**. On the next page, you'll see...

. . . what they all look like from the **back**.

Up and Down with Tigger

"What I mind about Tigger," Rabbit said,
 "Is not his jumping and pouncing.
What I mind about Tigger, to tell the truth,
 Is all that **up** and **down** bouncing."

"**Up** and **down**, **down** and **up**—
 I know it keeps him busy.
But all that **up** and **down** bouncing
 Is making *me* quite dizzy!"

UP goes
  UP Christopher Robin's
UP   train.

Where will it go
when
it gets
to the top?

DOWN
   DOWN
      DOWN again!

Kite Flight

Who's flying a kite?
Piglet and Roo.

The Kite is **up**—
and Roo is, too!

"Let go!" cries Piglet.
"I'm here to catch!"

And **down** comes Roo,
in a blueberry patch.

Smooth and Rough

As **smooth** as a ride down a slippery slide.

As **rough** as a bumpy wagon ride.

Top and Bottom

The Honey Pot Puzzle

Pooh and Piglet were on their way to visit Christopher Robin. Christopher Robin had been away, but now he was back. So they were bringing him "welcome home" presents.

Piglet was bringing a fresh carrot which Rabbit had given him from his carrot patch. And Pooh was bringing a pot of his very best honey.

On the way, Pooh suddenly stopped and sat down. "I'm worried about this honey," he said.

"It looks fine to me," Piglet replied. "It's a very nice pot indeed. And it's quite full of honey."

"That," said Pooh, "is the trouble. There's honey on **top**. We can see that. But how do we know it goes all the way down? How do we know there's honey on the **bottom**?"

Piglet scratched his ear. Then he scratched his nose. He tried hard to understand what Pooh was saying.

With a sigh, Pooh Bear scooped out some of the honey. "I'd better make *sure*," he said, as he tasted it.

"Ah," said Pooh, "that's honey all right. The whole **top** is honey. But I still don't know about the **bottom**. And there's only one way to find out."

Pooh took a big, drippy scoop of delicious honey. He smacked his lips. Then he took another scoop. And another. And another.

Soon Pooh Bear looked into the pot and smiled. "Well, *that's* settled. The honey went all the way down. Right to the **bottom**. I'm glad I solved the puzzle!"

Piglet looked into the empty honey pot. "You solved it all right—but now there's nothing left for Christopher Robin!"

Winnie-the-Pooh looked very unhappy.

"Oh, dear," he said. "Oh, my! Piglet, do you think—could we—perhaps—might we *both* give Christopher Robin your carrot, for his welcome home?"

"A good idea," nodded Piglet. "I'll give him the **top** part, and you can give him the **bottom**."

And off they went once more, very happily singing a welcome home Christopher Robin song.

Wet and Dry
Christopher Robin's Wash Day

Rub, scrub, rub!
Christopher Robin is
washing his socks.
Now the socks
are very **wet**.
How will he
get them **dry**?

Flip, drip, flip!
Christopher Robin
has hung
his **wet** socks
on the clothesline.
The warm sun
will **dry** them
soon!

In summer, a **hot** sun shines in the blue sky. Days and nights are very **hot**. On a **hot** day, Pooh likes to go on a picnic.

Winter days are very **cold**. There is **cold** icy rain. **Cold** winds blow. There are snowstorms, too. Then Rabbit gets out his sled and takes Roo for a ride.

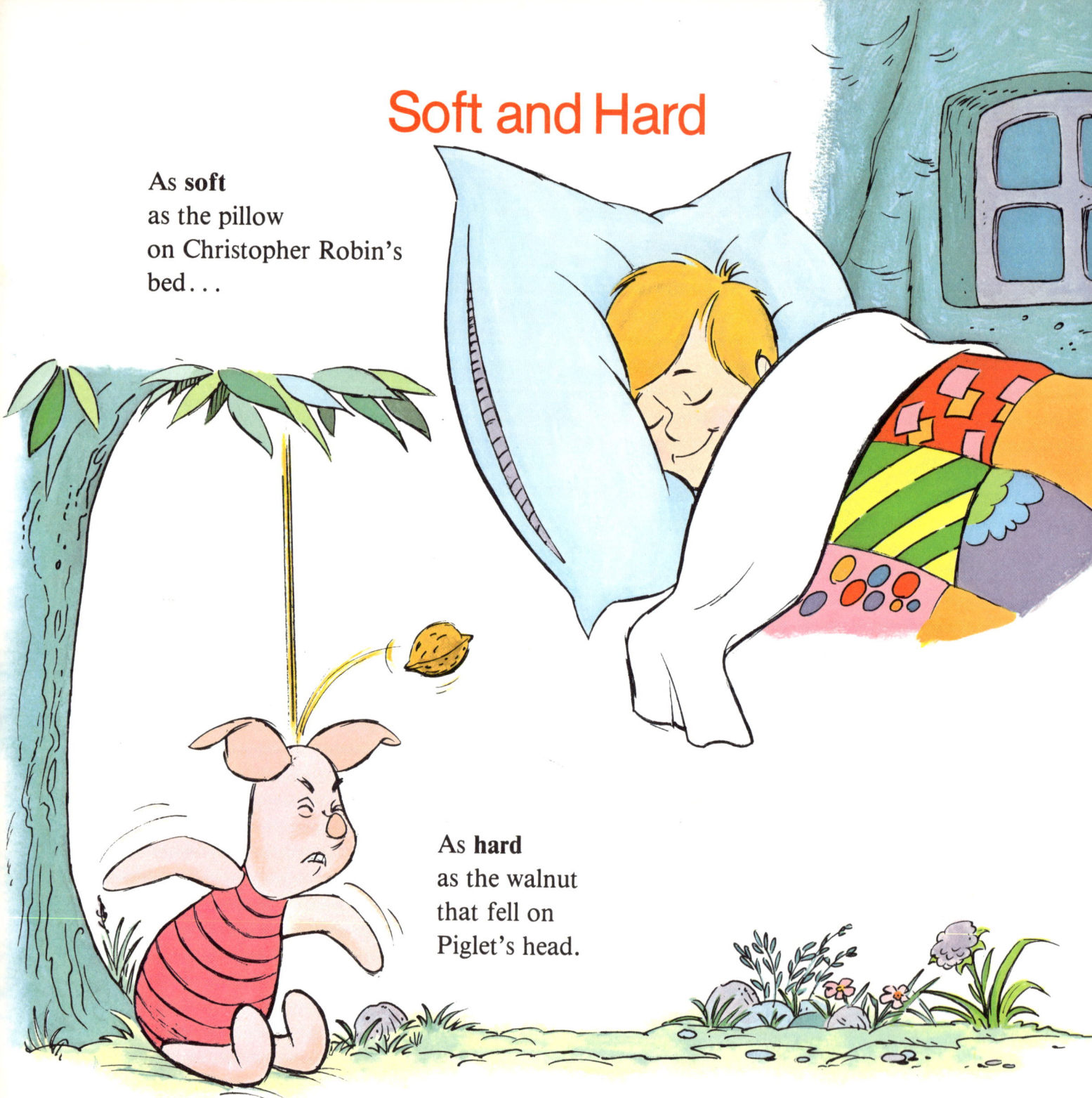

Soft and Hard

As **soft**
as the pillow
on Christopher Robin's
bed...

As **hard**
as the walnut
that fell on
Piglet's head.

Look all around your room. Can you find some **soft** things to touch? Can you find some **hard** things to touch?

Sick and Well

Who's **sick** in bed?
It's little Roo—
Now what will
Mother Kanga do?

She'll give him medicine.
It tastes funny—ick,
But it will make him
Well again—quick.

In and Out

A hollow log—
Hooray, what fun!
Let's follow
One another!

You go first,
I'll come next—
In one end
And **out** the other!

Over and Under

Winnie-the-Pooh is lost in the woods. Can you help him get to Christopher Robin's house? Using your finger, trace Pooh Bear's path **over** and **under** all the things he finds along the way.

Congratulations—you made it!

The Great Fence Mystery

Pooh and Piglet went for a stroll. Soon they came to a big fence. "What do you think is on the other side?" asked Pooh.

"I really wonder," replied Piglet.

"Let's solve this mystery," said Pooh. "I'll climb **over** and you crawl **under**."

Over went Pooh. **Under** went Piglet. Then they looked around. Do you know what they spied?

Right—the fence's other side!

The Carrot Patch

Rabbit is in his garden, digging up crispy, crunchy carrots. Some of the carrots are **big**. Some of the carrots are **little**. How many **big** carrots can you count? How many **little** carrots can you count?

Psst! There are 4 **big** carrots and 6 **little** carrots!

I'm BIG Pooh—

and I'm
LITTLE
Roo.

Old and New

Is Christopher Robin's wagon **new** or **old**?

Is Pooh's shirt **old** or **new**?

Are Roo's pencils **new** or **old**?

Are Piglet's boots **old** or **new**?

High and Low with Piglet

It was a gustery, blustery day. The wind blew and blew. Piglet sat on a tree stump in the wind. He watched the birds flying **high** and **low**.

"They fly so easily," thought Piglet, "just by flapping their little wings. I wish I could fly, too."

Piglet stood up on the tree stump and began to flap his arms. He flapped them **high** and **low,** imitating the birds. The wind blew harder and harder. Whoosh! Whoosh! Just then came the biggest and windiest gust of all. Whooooosh!

The wind lifted little Piglet **high, high, high** into the air, over the branches of a beech tree. The back of Piglet's shirt caught on the tip of a branch.

Piglet hung from the branch, **high** in the air. Soon, Owl came swooping toward him.

"Look at me, Owl!" cried Piglet. "I'm flying, just like you. Look how **high** I am!"

"My dear Piglet," sighed Owl, "I really *must* explain."

Owl perched on the branch next to Piglet. His weight made the branch wobble. Piglet shook loose.

Just then—whoosh!—another gust of wind came along. It caught little Piglet and carried him **low** toward the ground! And—ka-thump!—Piglet bumped right into Pooh who happened to come strolling along.

"Ooof!" said Pooh. "Hooosh!" he added.

"Sorry I bumped you, Pooh," cried Piglet. "I've been flying! **High** and **low**—just like the birds!"

Owl and Pooh looked at each other and smiled, as if to say, "Dear, silly Piglet. It was only the wind!"

As for Piglet, since he felt dizzy, he hurried home to rest. And to think about his great **high-low** adventure.

Mad and Glad

Pooh has a pot of honey.
Is he **mad** or **glad**?

Christopher Robin's little sailboat is broken.
Is he **mad** or **glad**?

Eeyore has just sat down in a bramble patch.
Is he **mad** or **glad**?

Piglet has a big new balloon.
Is he **mad** or **glad**?

Happy and Sad

Sometimes Eeyore is **happy,** and sometimes Eeyore is **sad**.
Can you tell which is the **happy** Eeyore, and which is the **sad** Eeyore?

Quiet and Noisy

As **quiet** as...
Winnie-the-Pooh humming a hum.

As **noisy** as...
Christopher Robin beating a drum.

First and Last
The Great Turn-Around Race

One day Christopher Robin and his friends decided to have a race. Eeyore didn't feel like running, so they made him the judge. The race would start at the bee tree and go all the way to Piglet's house.

"I'll surely come in **first**," said Rabbit with pride.

"And I," said Very Small Beetle, "will most likely be **last**."

Everyone lined up under the bee tree.

"On your marks, sort of," said Eeyore. "Get set, more or less. And now, I suppose—GO!"

Off went the runners. Rabbit quickly took the lead, holding **first** place. And Very Small Beetle fell far behind.

"I knew I'd wind up **last**," sighed Very Small Beetle.

Everyone ran as fast as possible. Rabbit ran the fastest of all and came in **first**, just as he expected. Very Small Beetle was the slowest of all and came in **last**, just as he feared.

But Eeyore felt sorry for Very Small Beetle.

"I am the judge," he announced, "so I hereby name this a turn-around race."

"A turn-around race!" squeaked Piglet. "What's *that*?"

Eeyore swished his tail in a very official way.

"In a turn-around race," he said, "everything is topsy-turvy. Also round-about-the-other-way. In other words, the one who comes in **first** loses. And the one who comes in **last** wins. So I hereby declare Very Small Beetle the winner!"

Everybody thought that was a fine idea, and they all cheered loudly. Even Rabbit. And Very Small Beetle decided that it was surely the very *best* race he had ever taken part in.

Day and Night

In the morning, the **day** begins. On a nice **day**, the sun is warm and bright. The sky is blue. Christopher Robin plays happily with Piglet and Pooh and Kanga and Roo.

At **night**, the sun goes down. Outside, everything is dark. **Night** is a time for looking at the stars and for sleeping. Good night, Christopher Robin. Sleep tight, Piglet and Pooh. Happy dreams, Kanga and Roo!